Ink flow

A Compilation of Poems

by Jan Baxter

Published by Jan Baxter 2007

ISBN: 978-0-6151-6008-5

Printed in the United States of America
1 2 3 4 5 6 7 8 9 0

Contact/Order at janikuspoetry@yahoo.com

PUBLISHER'S NOTE:

Gratitude

I want to thank my family for all of their love and support! Especially my mom, Betty, she's been my cheerleader for as long as I can remember and she's always been there to pick me up during hard times. Words cannot express my appreciation for her. I hope to be that person for someone else someday. Thanks to all my friends, particularly those closest to me; Rebecca, Clinton, Joel, Kathy, Robin, Anthony, Wade, Joy, Christi, Raquel, etc. As well as those I may not have specifically mentioned (too many to list them all), who have helped or inspired me along the way in my journey of life. Each person in my life has made some contribution to who I am as a person. Most importantly, I thank the Lord for all the blessings in my life and for giving me the ability to express myself in this way.

Dedication

This book is dedicated to my greatest friend on this entire earth; Rebecca. Whose encouragement and support have catapulted me past many barriers throughout my life. With her help, I have overcome many obstacles and realized my own personal potential. I draw strength from her and her words of encouragement. There's simply <u>no better</u> friend I could find! So, this is to you Rebecca, with all my love.

"A true friend is one soul in two bodies."
- Aristotle

Ink Flow-A Compilation of Poems

Table of Contents

Life

Life is like a tunnel,
Once you're in it
The whole ride through is dark.
But when you near the end,
You can see the light.
Yet, you still have doubts,
"Am I going to make it?"
"Will it be dark again?"
Then, just when you think
You've seen the light,
The ride is over.

Death

Horror known to all mankind.
The end of one life,
The start of anew.
Sins; will we go to Heaven?
Sins; will we go to Hell?
Do we make the choice?
Or does God choose for us?
Why have love if there
Must be death?
Who will know?
Death; horror known to all mankind.

Secret Admirer

Admiring you from afar,
Feeling as high as the stars.
Hoping fate will step in,
To make the good times begin.
So many things that I wonder,
Is this a spell that I am under?
Thinking of you all the time.
Wondering if you would be mine.
Wanting to know all about you,
To talk to you and hear your views.
Sharing your world and knowing you,
Something that I'd love to do.

Ups & Downs

Things may seem low, but nothing
Can go higher if it hasn't been low.
Even the sun starts at the bottom of the horizon.
Flowers start as sprouts low to the ground.
The higher they climb, the more
Beautiful they become.

<u>Good</u>

The good will prevail.
Hate is unacceptable.
Trust in myself, but no one else.
Life's too short for childish play.
I've much space in my heart,
Yet still I am betrayed.
Be true to myself.
My heart has no key, I leave it open,
For with a lock,
I only lock out myself.
Hurt is something I know too well.
But, the good will prevail.

<u>Something Greater</u>

To all who hear the unheard, those with the
knowledge we seek.
Not having to say a word,
Through our thoughts we speak.
Help us to comprehend,
What with our eyes, we cannot see.

Life Kills

Looking at life through a cracked glass lens,
Trying to figure out how it all transcends.
Just when you think it is almost clear,
Strikes another lightning bolt,
Piercing like a spear.
That's when you know exactly how it feels,
To be the victim that proves life kills.

Knight of Honor

Darkness across the hillside,
Stillness fills the air.
The enemy lurks within the night,
Not knowing where.

The sword of life at your side,
Strengthening, protecting.
Fear is not an option,
The adrenaline makes you sting.

Your honor is your pride and your
Pride you will not spare.
Blood is shed and lives are lost,
All your pride is there.

Jan Baxter

Victory will be celebrated,
You've made your King proud!
"The Knight of Honor!"
The villagers shout aloud.

If death should greet you today,
Darkness, you'd allow.

Choices

A gun, a vice, a bomb.
What will take the next one?
Lust, rage, hate,
When will it be too late?
Power, greed, glory,
Can you believe the "old man's story?"
Life, peace, friend.
We must not pretend.

Travelers

As we walk the road of life,
We find that things aren't
Always the way we'd like.

Still the road goes on and we

Must keep moving; through all
The hills and low-water crossings.
The journey continues.
Only when we've seen the map,
Can we read it.

Unwind

I took a drive to that lonely place.
With the breeze and the trees,
The moon and the stars.
To clear my mind and free my soul.
Let the nighttime silence take control.
Close my eyes and let it all go numb.
Pull every string until the knot's undone.
I open my eyes and take a deep breath…

Life's Web

In life and death,
All must travel on.
Where one sees clear,
Another sees color.
How many web dreams
Must we weave?

Jan Baxter

Before the circle
Is finally whole?

Inside or Out

Through our eyes, it sees.
Through our heart, it bleeds.
Through our arms, it reaches.
Through our minds, it teaches.
Through our desires, it seeks.
It is our soul that speaks.

Always There

Sometimes weak, sometimes strong.
Sometimes angry, sometimes calm.
Sometimes cold, sometimes warm.
On a clear day or during a storm.
When life is good or in despair,
Like the wind, I am always there.

Distant Heart

All my life I've dreamed of you,
Yet, your face I have not viewed.
Your name I still do not know.
Your image true, when will it show?
Sometimes I look up to the stars,
Somewhere under them, I know you are.
My soul is with you, night and day.
When finally we meet, what will I say?
Until the day my sunshine gleams,
Sweet dreams to you, my sweetest dream.

My Darling

From a distance my heart pines.
As bright as the sun, an aura around you
shines.
My mind interrupted with a vision of you here.
The electricity I feel!
I get chills when you're near.
Loneliness and desperation must be spared.
I can't wait 'til something between us is shared.

Internal Pain

Within my heart is a big black hole.
I've tried to mend it, but I've worn out my soul.
What I need is renewal, love and hope.
But everything I feel just seems like a joke.
My heart is real and my soul's already
wounded.

Wounded Soul

Fill the heart with honest love.
Share that wish and imagine the best.
Only to find no one understands.
Things start to change and your heart aches.
Emotional torture takes over and exhausts you.
The heart is still full with no place to go.
I don't know how to fix my wounded soul.

Inspire

If for nothing more than the idea,
That moment will come.
If for nothing more than the feeling,
Look how far you've come.
If for nothing more than you,
Be yourself and inspire!

Waiting for My Love

It's in the nighttime that I think of you most.
And in my lifetime I've been lonely way too
much.
Can't wait 'til you're near me & I'm holding
you close.
My heart will ache for you 'til I feel your touch.

(Chorus twice)
I'll be waiting for my love to come around

You're all I can think of that can soothe my soul.
I long for you truly, this hold is so strong.
How long will it be? That's what I need to
know.
You'll always be with me, to my heart you
belong.

(Chorus twice)
I'll be waiting for my love to come around.

Hole of the Heart

Can't be seen, but always here.
Searching eyes everywhere.

Jan Baxter

A Piece of me owns your name.
Inside I've not felt the same,
Since those times I miss the most.
The memories I hold to me close.
All I need is to make a new start,
To seal this hole that's in my heart.

<u>Direction</u>

Many hills, many storms,
This I have seen,
The summit and the sunshine,
That's where I've been.
Alone in my own darkness.
What could this mean?
Will all become clearer;
Once I turn on the light?
Because I am looking,
I know I will be fine!
I now see a map,
Instead of just lines.

<u>Passing</u>

Lift your head up to the sky,
There I go flying by.

I am the clouds, the wind, the trees.
Whatever you see, that is me.
I have my wings and have taken flight.
Hold all your memories very tight.
Someday we will fly together.
Until then, make your own life better.

The Wall

Two and a half centuries old.
Made of solid manmade concrete.
It is more that four feet thick.
A single dinner knife I hold,
For use this time, not to eat.
To make a doorway, that the trick.
Chipping away, more and more.
Sometimes feeling much too weak.
To this job, I must stick.
In order to pass through that door,
I must keep working for what I seek.
Knowing the time will not be quick.
It is me who has all control.
To make a new world my retreat.
And light my new candle's wick.
The wall must fall, this I know.
This concrete prison, I must defeat.
So all that is left is only a brick.

Jan Baxter

Champ of the Future

The smell of fuel,
The sound of power.
Around the track,
They go for hours.
Pushing, nudging,
Sliding, drafting.
Trading paint, tempers flaring.
Strategy is what he's crafting.
The pit crew's there,
Ready and waiting.
For that 14-second stop
He'll be making.
Out in front again,
Leaving them all behind.
The strength within
Him always shines.
Here it comes,
The checkered flag.
Always giving reason
For us to brag.
The thrill and excitement,
It's all about racing.
It's the great #8
They all are chasing!

Rebecca's Words

I want to watch you do it yourself.
I'll be there for your journey through the tunnel.
You can always look back at me, I am there.
To see you walk through that door, turn to me
and smile;
There with you, my heart will soar.

Throughout time

On our way to melting
Into our true form.
All of our experiences
Help us to transform.
Finally learning how to get to
Know the person that is you.

Spirit Guide

I call on the Great Spirit
To guide me.
To help me find my true path
And continue my journey.

My mind has been clouded,
My thoughts astray.
Without my horse,
I travel the wrong way.

From you, I ask for your strength,
Your calm and your assurance.
To lead me to the known
Peace within my soul.

From there I shall soar,
Like the Eagle up high.
With my steed I will rise
To find many roads ahead.

<u>Love's Gift</u>

Love is the gift we give each other,
When we know our hearts are drawn together.
We need each other, our support and our care.
We gain more strength through all we share.
Time is ours to make our way,
Beside one another is where we'll stay.
It is quite obvious for me to see,
That you are love's gift to me.

Best Friend

The strength you find and give to me,
Gets me through all that's in front of me.
Without question, you listen to me.
With honesty, no matter how it sounds,
You tell me things to help me settle down.
You pick up my spirits when no one else is
around.
You are the truest friend that I have found!
You never say just what I want to hear.
The truth hurts and we know that is clear!
Showing me every angle, you eliminate my
fears.
Without an oath, a promise, a creed.
You're always there when there's a need.
In my heart you've placed a seed.
As it grows like a tree,
I know now that I can and will succeed.
With all the love that you invest,
You are unlike all the rest.
You are my friend, yes, my best!

Jan Baxter

Simple Words Mean So Much

You always know how to say exactly the wrong
thing.
You always make me ask myself why I try.
The key being that I try.
I want you to be a part of my life
Yet I hate it when you are.
We are tied by blood but
The knot is always slipping.
I pull it tighter and you seem to loosen it.
It is a never-ending struggle,
For me, at least.
I wonder how it feels to not care.
To not feel what should be.
How can one heart be so cold and numb?
And the other is so hopeful & vulnerable?
Sometimes certain words do not need to be
said.
In most cases that is, 'I love you'.
In ours, it's the bitterness of the past.
The only part I have in that is
Being in the middle for no reason.
It shouldn't matter, it's over.
Life has moved on.
Why can't you?

Bitterness

Bitterness is a poison.
Eventually it will take effect;
Making your brain go haywire.
Then you loose all control.
Others distance themselves.
Life doesn't mean much anymore.
If you could just let the bitterness go,
It would fall away from you for good.
Unless you like the havoc it wreaks.
That may explain why it keeps going on.
Live your life in misery if you choose.
I refuse to succumb to bitterness myself.
I care too much about those around me.
I will not forfeit my loved ones.

The Dragon's Flight

Flying through the night,
Setting the night ablaze;
To light their way.

Flying cover where needed,
Risking yourselves;
Trying to keep them safe.

Jan Baxter

The great Dragon in the sky,
Soaring over;
Building their confidence.

With your mission done,
For those who couldn't;
You return home for them.

To make it worth it,
For you, for them;
We are all proud.

*In honor of my dad, Jerry Baxter, his AC-47, 'Puff
the Magic Dragon' 4th Air Commando Squadron,
Vietnam 1966-1967;
And for all who served, especially those that gave all.*

Mom

Things haven't always been the best
And I know I haven't been perfect.
I put you through a lot growing up.
My words and actions have hurt you,
I know, from time to time.

I can say I was a kid and didn't know better,

I can say I had my own issues I didn't
understand.
Nothing makes it okay to me now that I'm
grown.
My love for you is strong
And truer than any I've ever known.

I understand what you gave up for me,
And how you tried to keep my life good.
Even when there was no money,
I had a home, clothes and food.
Some say you spoiled me and maybe that's
true.

I know you wanted to help me.
To make up for my personal pain,
That even I didn't realize I had.
I've made bad choices and some good,
But you supported me no matter what.

Even when I lashed out,
You were there to hold me.
I know how hard you struggled,
And never once complained.
As long as we were together,
I think you felt complete.

No one knows me better than you,

You're the one I can tell all my secrets to.
You've seen me at my very worst,
When I was down and had no hope.
You never judge or compare me,
You only want what's best.

You've seen me at my best and we've shared
Many good times and laughs.
We have many more of these times ahead.
The pride we share is mutual.
I love you like no one else.

We have our disagreements, like everyone else.
But I never worry that we can't make up.
I know you'll always be there.
I'm trying to do better for you,
As I'm growing older.

I want to repay you for everything you've done.
No amount of money can equal that.
So I will do what I can to take care of you,
To make sure your life is good.

Thanks for being patient with me,
As I learn this thing called life.
I wouldn't be who I am without you.
I will struggle and life will still be hard,
But I know it can be done.

I'm grateful for every new day with you,
I hope for so many more.
I don't know what I'll do without you,
When that time comes.
My love for you will continue,
With each and every sun.

I ask that you forgive me,
For what I've said and done.
There's still times when
I don't think before I speak.
I acknowledge that and apologize.

No bond is stronger that mother and child.
I know this is true for you and me.
For you I would do anything.
Thanks to you, I am able to write this,
To express my heart to you.

Family Circle

Age has brought to me many things.
Now I feel what connection brings.
I've lived so far, as if alone.
I want to be near them to make my home.
The time has come to start my future.

Jan Baxter

My feelings of this are completely sure.
To settle in and share my life with them.
Missing so much makes my light grow dim.
My heart tells me I have to be near.
This epiphany is all too clear.
Even if the sky turns red and grass grows purple;
I am compelled to link with my family circle.

Accept Change

Change brings the renewal needed to let your soul free.
Time is relevantly irrelevant every now and then.
When is old, it's long and when it's short, it's new.
Positive or negative, change still must happen somewhere.
Renewal brings learning and expansion of thought.
Occasionally, time must be ignored and the facts enjoyed.
When it's good, you want longevity and when it's not, you want closure.

The only thing that's guaranteed is that nothing
is guaranteed.
Clarity is the gift gained from making life's
mistakes.
Looking back and seeing your mistakes is a sign
of growth.
Certain things in life grow more precious
everyday.
Age brings the wisdom to prioritize
appropriately.
The things you take for granted must be
cherished and preserved.
You can't wait too long or it will be too late.
Seize the chance to grab what's important while
you can.
Tomorrow can bring anything, good or bad.
Be in command of today, which alone may be
the change of a lifetime.
Free your soul and accept change when it's
here.

<u>Young Love Everlasting</u>

Your young love has brought you together.
Earn your trust and honor each other.
May loyalty and truth, take you far,

But always remember who each of you are.
To each other, you must give yourselves.
It's up to you and no one else.
Love will bring you through bad weather,
But you must work, to keep it together.
Hearts are soft and must be held carefully.
Words can be sharp, but also spoken
thoughtfully.
Always try to make your own silver lining.
Keep you hearts true and always smiling.
Like the warm glow the sun is casting,
Allow your love to be everlasting.

<u>Guiding Angels</u>

Life, like our mothers, teaches us many lessons.
Bringing us from grief when what we need is
peace.
When you feel all is lost, you have to count your
blessings.
The things that bring us down, we must let go
and release.
To two little angels, you now have to teach,
In a world where we don't always like how
we've been treated.

When the goal of being the better person seems
hard to reach,
Do everything you can to make sure the pain is
not repeated.
Call on the strength that we all know is inside
you.
Guide yourself and your life to the best place
you can.
Your angels will depend on everything that you
do.
As their beautiful mother, their future is in your
hands.
Life is what you make it and how you handle
your perception.
Make everyday a day you remember and
cherish forever.
Have faith in family and love and you'll go in
the right direction.
With all the love that you have, you'll get
through it all together.

Time to Go

Honor me, by remembering me,
As I will remember you and
All the times, together, we've had.

Jan Baxter

Every moment, I will cherish,
No matter if it was good or
Even if it was bad.
Each and every time you do,
For as long as time allows,
I will be there with you.
Hear me in that song,
See me in that picture,
Our connection will always be pure.
Distance is just a measure,
But not of our bond,
This bond we'll always treasure.
To go, I must, it is my time,
Know your place in my heart,
You will always shine.

<u>Reflection Garden</u>

We should all step back and take time to reflect.
What has our individual lives taught us?
Maybe it isn't quite what we expect.
Everyday is a gift, in this we must trust.
Good or bad, the days still come and go.
The sun will still rise with or without us.
We have to assure our legacy will grow.
Living each day as if it were our last is a must.

Around the corner, we'll never know what's
there.
Things can change without warning beyond our
control.
Sometimes there's no time for us to be
prepared.
We need to make our daily lives slow down,
To look more closely at the 'little things';
At times they are overlooked in our rush to get
around.
Be more in control of what our lives bring.
Share more time with the ones we may take for
granted.
Our time together is not guaranteed.
We need to nurture the seeds we've planted;
Not always worry about clearing the weeds.

Rainbow Deserved

Where's my rainbow after the rain?
Has the storm fully passed?
A break is what I need.
I am flooded and feel like I'm drowning.
My strength has weakened
And my faith has been wounded.
How do I find new hope everyday?

I've tried to do all the right things.
Then I find there's something else waiting,
Waiting to take from me again.
I almost have nothing left but
Still I am required to give.
I want to be productive and
Provide for what is necessary.
I've not felt this broken for having
Given up so much for good intentions.
I know in the long run it is worth it.
It's hard to keep that in mind,
When times are so hard and
I feel so helpless.
I don't want to let anyone,
Including myself, down.
Partly for pride and partly of fear.
Where do I go from here?
It's not in my control and that's hard.
I can only wait and hope
As each day passes and more
Things become needed without
A source to provide them.
I am trying to stay sane and
Preserve some dignity.
I don't want anything handed to me
But I do need a door to open
That allows me to walk through
And take hold of my life and purpose again.

Jan Baxter

Some say it can only get better now,
But it still keeps steadfastly falling.
When will the rain stop?
Where is my rainbow?

<u>Legacy</u>

A daughter, grand-daughter, sister, niece, aunt
and friend;
That's what, in this wonderful life, I have been.
I have lived each role the best way that I could.
I know these relationships have made my life
good.
Those I have lost along my path, I've missed so
much!
Now's my chance to reunite and be with the
whole bunch.
Those still here, I wait to see again, some other
time.
A legacy of words and memories is what I leave
behind.
My best form of expression has always been my
words.
I leave these and more for you and hope to be
heard.

Be there for one another through good times
and bad.
Don't spend too much of your precious time
being sad.
Remember me with smiles and laughter in your
heart.
As long as you do, we will never be too far
apart.

You **With Me**

Sometimes I lose my direction, but *You're*
always there to steer me back.
Anytime I ask, *You* answer me, even if I don't
always hear it right away.
I haven't always listened closely to what *You've*
had to say to me.
Sometimes I didn't even realize it was *You*
talking to me when I heard *You*.
I guess I just thought it was my imagination or
just wishful thinking maybe.
I wondered why I never got the answers I
expected & sometimes none at all.
I thought I was not good enough or was being
punished in some way.

Then someone spoke just the right words to me
one day on my porch.
I was sitting there lonely & trying to find what
it was that I was missing.
It was as if *You* were truly speaking through
them directly to me.
Everything was so clear & poignant to my
situation on that October day.
I was touched so deeply & afterward was just
gleaming with awe & gladness.
I could not get over how I felt & the thought
that I may have just seen *You* in person.
Even though I know it was another person, I
also know *You* were there with me.
After that day, I seemed to hear & see *You*
everywhere talking just to me.
At least that's how it seemed to me at the time
& even now looking back.
Things that had nothing to do with me, had
everything to do with me.
As I have drawn closer to *You* & begun to grow
with *You* in my heart;
I have come to realize a lot of things about my
life & myself.
Also, I know that *You* have been there listening
to me all along,
I just didn't understand *You* and how *You* were

responding to me.
So many things about *You* that I had read &
been told before, I didn't understand.
I do understand so much more now & am
learning more every single day.
I know that it's up to *You* how things turn out,
You decide, not me.
I know that if I live my life how *You* want me to,
You'll provide everything I need.
I know that when I speak to *You, You* do hear
me even if I can't hear a response.
I know my struggles are a part of my growth &
learning in life.
I know & rejoice that for the rest of my life &
forever, it's *You* with me!

Baxter, the Hunting Rifle

This old family gun, given to you to help hone
your skills,
It has drawn the blood of all your family's first
deer kills.
From Papa Baxter, Uncle JR to your Dad, Billy
& your Cousin Shawn,
Now, Cody, down to you they pass this old rifle
on.

It's now your turn to add to its history & get
<u>your</u> first deer.
Then you'll pass it down to continue this
tradition for years and years.

<u>Mindy, Our Miracle</u>

To our family, we've been given a great miracle.
Not once, but twice we've been blessed by it.
First, a healthy baby girl, Reagan Leanne;
Second, her mother, Mindy's life returned to us.
In shock, we were told of her heart's condition.
Beside ourselves, we couldn't image how this
could be.
So young and expecting a new beautiful baby.
It seems impossible, crazy! What can we do?!
We asked everyone we knew for prayers and
support.
We prayed together and we prayed separately.
Our hearts were on the floor, our minds in
turmoil.
Comprehending it all was the greatest
challenge.
At first the doctors didn't think it was going
well.

The strength in our faith and in her soul kept
fighting.
Slowly things were changing and she was
responding.
Every little movement elated us completely.
I couldn't wait to hear her voice, just one little
word.
That would assure me she was coming back to
us.
That day came and I felt such relief and
thankfulness.
From there she continued to improve everyday.
Now she's home and living life again with her
family.
We are all truly blessed for this life-giving
miracle.
We'll never be able to give thanks equivalent to
her life.
But we will be thankful for the rest of all of
ours.

Tomorrow's Promise

On earth, tomorrow is promised to no one.
Focus on today's journey;
And the great things we can do.

Trust that the Lord has a plan.
Our faith will show us heaven.
He will give us the eternal oasis,
He's promised us through faith.
We won't always know why
We go through what we do in life.
He is always there, silently guiding us.
Sometimes we know when, often we don't.
He knows our pain and hears our pleas.
In His time we will be exalted.
As we wait, we must keep our faith strong.
We truly can handle everything He gives us.
He knows this better than we do.
As long we continue to believe;
Our tomorrow's promised in heaven, next to
Him.

Texas Home

My thoughts are far off,
As I miss my home.
Sometimes it's so hard
To understand what I've done.

I've left my heart there,
And sometimes my head.

Such great memories are there
On those streets that I've tread.

I never thought I'd miss
That hot Texas sun;
But that is my home,
It's where I'm from.

I dream of being back there
With all those I've left.
My heart sinks inside me
And I find myself distressed.

It seems like forever,
That I've been away.
I find it so hard here
To make myself stay.

Even though I'm surrounded
By those that I love.
I have to pray for strength
From the One up above.

Sometimes I feel guilty
That here I'm not as content.
Even though I feel that
By God I was sent.

I miss all the simple things,
The wildflowers along the roads;
The water from Barton Springs,
So refreshing and cold.

The ones I have trusted and
Kept me from feeling alone.
I just miss so very much,
My sweet, warm Texas home.

www.ingramcontent.com/pod-product-compliance
Lightning Source LLC
Chambersburg PA
CBHW022343040426
42449CB00006B/689